Jamaica

BONECHI & LMH PUBLISHING LTD

© Copyright 2009 by Casa Editrice Bonechi - Florence - Italy
E-mail: bonechi@bonechi.it

© Copyright 2009 by LMH Publishing Ltd.

Publication created by *Casa Editrice Bonechi* Publication manager: *Monica Bonechi*
Photographic research by the *Editorial Staff of the Casa Editrice Bonechi* and *LMH Publishing*
Graphic design and layout: *Massimo Francalanci, Elena Nannucci*
Cover: *Elena Nannucci* Editing: *Mattia Mela, Patrizia Fabbri*

Printed in Italy by *Centro Stampa Editoriale Bonechi* - Sesto Fiorentino

The photographs used in this publication belong to the archive of
Casa Editrice Bonechi and were taken by:
Andrea Fantauzzo, Paolo Giambone, Andrea Innocenti.

Other contributors:
Jamaica Tourist Board (courtesy of): p. 95 (background);
Atlantide/Guido Cozzi: p. 47 above;
Corbis: p. 36/37 (photo by Robert Landau);
Delroy A. Whyte-Hall: p. 10/11, 12-15, 18 below, 19, 20 above and below, 21 above and below,
26, 27, 28 centre right and below, 30/31, 31 centre, 35 (the three small photos), 37 (the four
small photos), 42/43, 43 below, 44, 45, 46 (the two photos below), 47 (the two photos below),
49 centre and below right, 50, 51, 57 above right and left, 60, 62-67, 70-73, 74 below, 76,
77 above and below left, 80 above, 81, 83, 92/93;
Getty Images: p. 3 (photo by Dorling Kindersley), 8 above (photo by Mike Hewitt) and below
(photo by Ben Radford), 9 (photo by Stuart McClymont), 32 (photo by Philip Coblentz),
33 (photo by Philip Coblentz), 34/35 (photo by Cris Haigh), 48 (photo by Graham Wiltshire),
49 above (photo by Evening Standard), 78 above (photo by Oliver Benn),
88 below (photo by Michael Gilbert);
Leonardo Olmi: p. 88 above, 89-91;
LMH Publishing (courtesy of): p. 20 above left and centre, 21 centre, 28 centre left, 38/39,
43 above, 49 below left, 54, 55, 80 below.

The publisher apologies for any omissions and is willing to make amends
with the formal recognition of the author of any photograph subsequently identified.

ISBN 978-88-476-1664-6

www.bonechi.com

INTRODUCTION

EARLY DAYS

'The fairest isle that eyes have ever seen.' So Columbus described Jamaica when he returned to Spain in 1494 after his second voyage to the West Indies. Crumpling a piece of paper, he flung it on the floor at the feet of King Ferdinand and Queen Isabella, showing the towering mountains which so impressed voyagers sailing to safe harbour on the island. Although Columbus christened the island St. Jago when he claimed it for Spain, it become known by a form of the original Arawak name: Xaymaca, *land of wood and water*. The Arawaks were fitting inhabitants of this beautiful island.

SPANISH SETTLEMENT

The first town in Jamaica was Sevilla la Nueva, built in 1510 on the North Coast near what is now St. Ann's Bay. Within easy reach of Cuba and Hispaniola, it was a logical site for the town, but only fourteen years after it was founded the inhabitants abandoned it for the southern plains. Fewer than ten of all the children born there had survived, so it is probable that settlers were searching for a healthier environment.

The new town, Villa de la Vega, today **Spanish Town**, had access to two good harbours. The main activity of the colonists was supplying fresh provisions to passing ships and exporting hides and lard to Cuba.

As early as 1517, the Spaniards began to bring in slaves from Africa to work in the fields. This backwater of the great Spanish empire drifted into a quiet, self-contained life, concerned with its own disputes and trade. At most, the Spanish population was 1,500, a small enough number to ensure continuous feuding.

By the mid-1600s, Spanish Town had become a very attractive town featuring four or five hundred houses, five or six churches or chapels, a cathedral and one monastery. There was a Jewish burial ground. Around the coast were a few towns, such as **Port Antonio**, **Montego Bay**, and **Savanna la Mar**, and scattered settlements.

In May, 1655, a fleet of thirty-eight ships sailed into **Kingston Harbour**. The English had come to take over. Jamaica's Spanish days had ended.

BRITISH CAPTURE

When the English troops marched into Spanish Town, they found it deserted with nothing left to loot. Enraged, they destroyed many buildings; then, having gained nothing, they prepared to wait until they were recalled to England. Supplies ran short, they had wantonly killed most of the cattle the Spanish had left behind, and fever and famine soon set in, reducing their numbers drastically. Those who survived refused to plant crops, fearing that if they did so they would be compelled to remain on the island. They were constantly attacked by the slaves the Spaniards had freed, even in Spanish Town itself. Those freed Africans were to become the Maroons, the name coming from the Spanish *cimarron*, or 'wild'.

A NEW COLONY

Settlers arrived in surprising numbers from England and other West Indian islands. They set up plantations, began to import slaves from Africa, and those who came from Barbados introduced the production of sugar.

King Charles II came to the English throne, and he too encouraged settlement in Jamaica. With increasing prosperity came a civilian government with a Governor representing the King, an appointed Council, and an elected Assembly.

The small fortified town of **Port Royal** was built for defence at the tip of the peninsula almost enclosing Kingston Harbour. It became the richest and most wicked city in the western hemisphere. Its wealth was brought in by the buccaneers who, with their leader Henry Morgan, had been encouraged to make Port Royal their base. Jamaica was thus protected against the Dutch and Spanish. The buccaneers attacked the Spanish on land and sea at every opportunity. They brought their plunder into Port Royal and squandered it.

INTRODUCTION

THE EIGHTEENTH CENTURY

During the 1700s, Jamaica was repeatedly in danger of attack. First the pirates had to be wiped out. The death of Calico Jack Rackham in 1728 on what is still called Rackham's Cay in Kingston Harbour ended that threat. Then, as the European wars of the 18th century spread to the valuable islands of the West Indies, Jamaica was constantly on the alert.

The end of the 18th century brought the beginnings of change which would permanently affect Jamaica. The system of slavery was being questioned both on economic and humanitarian grounds. The missionary activities of the Nonconformist churches were spreading Christianity among the slaves and, in spite of determined opposition from West Indian landowners, the movement for the abolition of slavery was gaining ground in England.

EMANCIPATION AND AFTER

In the English parliament, the anti-slavery movement finally prevailed. The first effects felt in the West Indies came with the abolition of the slave trade in 1807. This, however, did not improve the conditions of the slaves in bondage. With talk of freedom in the air and the knowledge that the planters were resisting emancipation, unrest among the slaves began to grow. Many believed that freedom had already been granted but that the slave owners were keeping it from them. The inevitable outburst came during Christmas week, 1831, near Montego Bay.

The plantation owners had been right when they contended that freedom for the slaves would ruin them. Deprived of free labour, many of them were unwilling to try new methods of sugar production, and absentee landowners in particular often preferred to let their properties fall into ruin rather than change their ways. Many ex-slaves left the estates and set up free villages in the hills, to become an independent peasantry which is the backbone of Jamaica today. Estates which continued to produce sugar used indentured labour from India or China, but it was difficult to compete with the beet sugar being produced in Europe.

Jamaica sank into a slow decline. Hardship was increased by a series of droughts. In 1865, the Morant Bay Rebellion flared out, aroused by the unfeeling arrogance of the authorities. Led by Paul Bogle, the rebels killed some fifteen whites including the Custos of the parish of St. Thomas.

Martial Law was declared and the rising was put down with the utmost severity on orders by the notorious Governor Eyre. Over 430 men and women of the peasantry were killed, more than 600 were flogged and 1,000 homes destroyed. Paul Bogle was hanged in **Morant Bay** and so was George William Gordon, a Kingston merchant and member of the Assembly, for his alleged role in the rebellion. Both of these men are now numbered among Jamaica's National Heroes.

In the panic of the aftermath, members of the elected Assembly gave up their independent powers and Jamaica became a Crown Colony, governed directly from London. By abdicating the responsibilities which the Assembly had struggled to hold for 200 years, the members passed the problems of Jamaica over to the British government which soon began to introduce reforms. One important change took place in 1872 when the seat of government was moved from Spanish Town to Kingston.

Two new developments contributed to improving conditions in Jamaica at the end of the 19th century. One was the beginning of migration in search of short or long term work. The second innovation was the export of bananas.

THE TWENTIETH CENTURY

With the beginning of the 20th century, Jamaica could hope to look forward to some degree of stability and prosperity. Too soon it was faced with its first disaster, the earthquake of 1907. The First World War presented the next crisis. Thousands of Jamaicans volunteered to fight for Britain, as they did in the Second World War. Jamaica was affected by the Depression in the 1930s, and the banana industry was ruined by disease. The problems of a rapidly increasing population added to the discontent. In 1938, riots developed from a strike by sugar workers in **Westmoreland** and there were serious disorders in Kingston. Out of the turmoil came the first effective trade unions in the island, and the two major political parties joined forces with those unions. Alexander Bustamante led the Jamaica Labour Party while his cousin, Norman Wash-

ington Manley, formed the more leftist People's National Party. Both men were powerful figures. They alternated in the political leadership of the island, but both worked towards preparing Jamaica for independence in 1962.

The Constitution of Jamaica guaranteed free elections, freedom of speech, freedom of worship and freedom of movement for all citizens.

During the 1970s, industrial expansion, especially the development of the bauxite industry, contributed to economic growth, but the prosperity did not benefit all. Once more, the increasing population put pressure on the society. Migration was becoming increasingly difficult, and unemployment was rising.

THE FUTURE

More recently, Jamaica has enjoyed a long period of growth and development that shows no sign of slowing down. The country's business dealings with the United States and neighbour countries in the Caribbean permit her to market her agricultural products and bauxite and aluminium (for years, the island's major exports). The driving sector of the Jamaican economy is, however, tourism - in both economy and luxury versions - which offers visitors the possibility to enjoy the island's beauty spots and valorises its potential for future generations.

INTRODUCTION

SPORTS

A nation isn't made of just history and economy, but also of culture, traditions, sports . . . all the every-day business that makes one people unique among others.

Sports is one of Jamaica's principal resources, but not just as a draw for visitors. The commitment of many professional athletes has won world-level recognition for the country with significant victories in various disciplines.

The national **football** team, nicknamed **Reggae Boyz**, plays an important role in the Caribbean area. Many of its athletes play for United States and English teams.

Cricket, an English legacy, is a popular sport in Jamaica. Over the years Jamaican cricket has produced excellent international-level players and the Jamaican side's stadium in the capital is enormous, the largest in the entire Caribbean.

Another vaunt of Jamaican professional sports is its record in **track** and **field**, a specialty in which Jamaican athletes have won an enviable array of Olympic medals and an impressive series of victories in both men's and women's events.

Sherone Simpson, Olympic gold medallist, sprints to a win in the 4 x 100 metres relay.

*The dynamism of English and Jamaican athletes immortalised during a **cricket match**.*

RASTAFARIAN MOVEMENT

Rastas belong to a religious cult which originated in Jamaica in the 1930s and which is still spreading today.

They see themselves as exiles from Africa, in Babylonian captivity, descendants of Ethiopian kings. For them, the late Emperor Haile Selassie I of Ethiopia is divine, and that divinity is unaffected by his death. When Haile Selassie visited Jamaica in 1966, the thousands who went to meet him at the airport swept through the security and on to the tarmac. Overwhelmed at the sight of the vast throng surrounding his plane, Haile Selassie refused to leave it until he was convinced that he was in no danger. He rode triumphantly into Kingston through the largest crowd ever to greet a foreign visitor. In spite of the Emperor's insistence that he was indeed human, nothing has ever been able to shake the Rastas' faith in his divinity. One of his titles, Lion of Judah, symbolises his power for them. The lion constantly appears in their art and is even suggested in the flowing manes of hair.

A significant part of Rastafarian life is spent in meditating over the Bible and discussing its true meaning. It is the essential guide to their beliefs and daily life. From it they have developed the strict ethical code and social organisation by which they live, and even their mainly vegetarian, salt-free, diet which they call *ital* food.

Two aspects of Rasta life, however, are definitely non-Biblical. One is their assertion of African pride and continuity, perhaps the result of the parallel influence of Garveyism in the Thirties. The other, which constantly leads to conflict with the authorities, is the use of *ganja*, or marijuana, as an integral part of their ritual. The 'holy weed' is smoked in a shared pipe in the ceremony, but many Rastas smoke it, illegally and rolled into spliffs, at any time. The true Rastafari is outstandingly honest and peaceful. His greeting is Peace and Love. Since he asks for nothing beyond the bare essentials of life, his needs are few. Unfortunately, the Rastas' appearance and seemingly unstructured life provide good cover for criminal elements whose activities harm the image of the genuine followers.

***Dreadlocks**, a symbol of the Rastafarian movement, have become a global fashion beyond any strictly religious connotation.*

MONTEGO BAY

The name **Montego Bay** conjures up romantic pictures of tropical vacations, but its origin is definitely unromantic. It comes from the Spanish *manteca*, the lard the local people used to supply to passing ships.

Montego Bay had a slow start in Jamaican history. The earliest settlers found the bay too exposed to the threat of attacks from pirates and they feared the Maroons in the wild **Cockpit Country** nearby.

But by the great days of sugar in the eighteenth century, Montego Bay and the parish of **St. James** were sharing fully in prosperity, as the Great Houses of the area testify today. The town also developed a tradition of independence. Far away from the capital in Spanish Town, it tended to manage its own affairs. Montego Bay is still referred to, half jokingly, as The Republic by the rest of Jamaica. High-rise hotels cluster

*A lazy day in the sun for bathers on Montego Bay's **Doctor's Cave Beach**.*

together within the town, while more spacious resorts spread out east and westwards. Even the **Bogue Islands**, a small group of offshore cays, have been captured and joined to the mainland to form **Montego Freeport** with holiday villas and a hotel beyond.

Columbus called the bay the **Gulf of Good Weather**. Even by Jamaican standards, there seems to be more sunshine here than anywhere else, as well as the best sailing conditions in the islands. Montego Bay is a yachtsman's delight, and the Montego Bay Yacht Club is widely known for its generous hospitality. Regattas are often held and there is a tough Round-the-Island race,

but the highlight is the MoBay Race (or Pinneaple Cup), an international event where the celebrations when the winner is announced are matched only by the excitement of the race itself.

One of Montego Bay's beauty spots is the **Old Fort**. Three of the original 17 cannons still remain and the solidly built powder magazine is still intact. It is known to have been there since 1752, but its history does not match its impressive appearance. The guns were fired only twice, and on one of those occasions one of them exploded, killing the gunner. The second time, they fired on a British ship. Fortunately, but not surprisingly, they missed, and have never been used since.

DOWNTOWN

In the centre of Montego Bay is **Sam Sharpe Square**. As in Kingston, the Square was once the Parade, recalling military days. Later it became **Charles Square** and finally it was named after the rebel slave leader and present day national hero who was hanged on the square. In the north-west corner of the Square near to the old lock-up called **The Cage** is a group of bronze figures dedicated to the memory of Sam Sharpe. This unusual work by a Jamaican artist, Kay Sullivan, captures the intensity of the response which Sharpe's preaching must have drawn from his hearers. Whether tourists come in by cruise ship or plane, they will find that Montego Bay has much to offer: fine beaches, water sports, tours, entertainment, a lively night-life and good shopping. Attractive shopping malls have the best of in-bond shopping with a wide range of luxury goods. Locally designed resort wear rivals anything that can be bought abroad; straw work and souvenirs can be found in the **Crafts Market**. Inevitably, the *mento* singers will appear. Although they sing calypso, which is an import from Trinidad, *mento* is the true Jamaican form, and they can improvise a song to suit their listener on the spot.

On the facing page, attractions and restaurants at Montego Bay. Clockwise from the top: Pier One, Breezes Hotel, Margaritaville, Doctor's Cave Beach, and the Coral Cliff Casino and Gaming Lounge. Below, the Civic Centre, a national-level cultural attraction, and (bottom) the City Centre Building, a Mecca for shopping in Montego Bay.

CRAFT MARKET

The perfect way to pass the time between one dip and the next is a stroll among the stalls at the Montego Bay **Craft Market**. Here you can enjoy a chat with local artisans, purchase a unique craft item to take home as a souvenir, or simply bask in the thousands of colours and forms that animate this picturesque corner of the city.

DOCTOR'S CAVE

Dr. Alexander McCatty persuaded his patients that the best way to recover their health was sea bathing, preferably from his own beach with its cave and spring. In 1906, he opened up his beach as a semi-public bathing club, and people began to come, first from Kingston and then from overseas. By the 1920s, when an English doctor claimed that the spring had therapeutic powers, Montego Bay had become established as a resort for the wealthy who came to bathe at Doctor's Cave Beach and to enjoy a long winter vacation.

Although the doctor's cave has long since disappeared, Doctor's Cave Beach is still a top attraction, and well worth the small fee charged for its use. The town has been much transformed since Dr. McCatty's day.

LANDING ON THE SEA

In Jamaica, airport-to-beach time is reduced to a minimum. The approach to the **Sir Donald Sangster International Airport**, Jamaica's largest, is over the transparent Caribbean waters; the air terminal, which serves thousands of visitors every year, links Jamaica with the other Caribbean islands and the airports of the world.

GOVERNOR'S COACH TOUR

A tour with a difference is the **Governor's Coach Tour**, a train ride forty miles into the Jamaican countryside, part of it through wild **Cockpit Country**. The tour ends at a sugar estate famous for its rum.

After a picnic lunch by the river, the travellers return, stopping on the way at one station to pick up the dresses that some of them ordered to be made on the way down that morning.

*A dream-sequence sunset over palms and the beach near **Montego Bay**.*

BIRD FEEDING STATION

At **Rocklands** just west of the town is a bird feeding station. The Jamaican Doctor Birds, streamer-tailed humming birds, are so tame that they come to be fed. A bird-watcher's delight.

Golfing in Montego Bay

TRYALL

18-hole, par-72: one of the most beautiful golf courses in the Caribbean. With its carefully-groomed fairways and greens, space galore and luxury services, **Tryall** is also famous for its caddies: courteous, expert, and highly professional. A word of advice for visitors wanting to spend a day at Tryall: make your reservations well in advance! Besides attracting new clients every day, Tryall boasts a permanent clientele of players who make the trip to Jamaica for the sole pleasure of a game on this course.

*On these pages, some views of the two **golf courses**.*

WHITE WITCH

The **White Witch Golf Course** is built right on the sea. Sixteen of its 18 holes afford views of the Caribbean Sea, whose turquoise is the perfect counterpoint to the green of the fairways. Par-71 over 6,719 yards, the course grounds abound with activities and services complementing the enchantment of its splendid location. And what's more, it's only ten minutes from its proprietor **Ritz-Carlton Hotel**.

True golf-lovers will be pleased to learn that the **Rose Hall Resort Area** offers a total of 54 holes on its constituent courses.

Hotels in Montego Bay

HALF MOON

A *400-acre estate is the setting for one of the Caribbean's loveliest hotels. Palms, crystalline waters, and colonial style are the prime elements that strike the visitor on arrival, but what is really surprising about the **Half Moon** is its carnet of activities: golf on its par-72 course, **Dolphin Lagoon**, 51 swimming pools, 13 tennis and squash courts, basketball and volleyball courts, spa services, and*

many others, including a space for the youngest set named for the most famous trickster in Jamaican folk tales: 'Anansi' the Spider.

RITZ-CARLTON

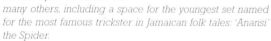

S *ited in the exclusive **Rose Hall area**, the **Ritz-Carlton Resort** features golf courses and spas in 5000 acres of well-tended coastal land. Just 15 minutes from **Sangster International Airport**, this luxury resort offers an enormous variety of aquatic sports facilities and other recreational activities, five restaurants that will tickle even the most demanding palates in elegant, seductive surroundings, and made-to-measure services for satisfying any client.*
And naturally, there is no lack of activities for children, from the creative workshops to group activities, to reading, and to beach games and sand castles.

SANDALS

S *andals is a synonym of luxury: five restaurants featuring international menus, bars, and elegant night-clubs, and an unlimited selection of vacation possibilities, whether you're looking for non-stop emotions or total do-nothing relaxation. If your wish list includes a romantic wedding on the beach and a honeymoon just a step away from the church, here's your answer. **Sandals Montego Bay** offers its clients a wedding chapel on the water with the Caribbean sun sparkling overhead.*
All the comforts of a European-style spa and lazy strolls through the marvels of this immense estate: Sandals promises its guests unforgettable moments in a paradise where chance meetings are likely to blossom into lasting friendships.

ROSE HALL

Ten miles east of **Montego Bay**, the most famous Great House in Jamaica stands on a low rise looking out to sea. **Rose Hall** is part of the island's history, the home of a lasting legend and extraordinary proof of the determination of American millionaire John Rollins who, in the early 1970s, restored the house to its early magnificence. Two centuries before, James Palmer, a rich landowner and Custos of the **Parish of St. James**, had built the house for his wife Rosa at the immense cost of 30,000 pounds sterling. It replaced an earlier Rose Hall on his wealthy wife's property where she had lived for some twenty years. He was her fourth husband. The house he built was a monument to the extravagant way of life of the great Jamaican planters. Solidly built of cut stone and mahogany, it had a handsome double staircase which swept up past the arches of the ground floor storage rooms to the terraces and reception rooms above. The house was, of course, furnished with the greatest elegance.

Mrs. Rosa Palmer had twenty more years of happy married life at Rose Hall. Her memorial in **St. James Parish Church** in Montego Bay was the work of one of the most famous English sculptors of the day and lists her many virtues. Her husband remarried, died in 1797, and from then on the story of Rose Hall becomes an inextricable tangle of recorded facts, legend, mystery, and folk memory.

The result is the Legend of Annie Palmer, the White Witch of Rose Hall. Even Rosa Palmer herself, with her four husbands, was once thought to have been the White Witch. But there was a real Annie Palmer, wife of James Rose Palmer who inherited the property in 1820. It was she who was found strangled in her bed in 1833. Whether she was murdered by a lover who feared he was losing her favour or by desperate slaves was never established. And the mystery surrounding her death gradually shrouded the whole of her life at Rose Hall. She was said to have had a habit of dressing as a man and riding over the property at night, cracking her whip at any slave she found; she is said to have inflicted extreme tortures on the slaves and to have enjoyed watching them suffer. When a slave girl was found guilty of attempting to poison her and was executed in Montego Bay, Annie Palmer forced a suspected accomplice to carry the girl's head in a basket back to Rose Hall

where it was placed on a pole as a warning. Yet there is no trace in the court records of Annie Palmer ever having been involved in a case in Montego Bay. Husbands and lovers disappeared. Indelible marks on a bedroom floor are the bloodstains of the lover she stabbed. She became a mistress of Obeah and held the souls of her slaves in her power. But the death of her first husband was recorded, and at least one of her supposed lovers was known to have left the island. So the mixture of legend and fact continues. It is true, though, that no slaves on her property would dig her grave and that the mason who raised the square pile of masonry two feet high above it refused cash payment but accepted a bull-calf.

*Painstaking restoration has returned the facade (facing page) and interiors (above and left) of the **Rose Hall House** to their original look.*

GREENWOOD
GREAT HOUSE

East of **Montego Bay**, on the border of **St. James** and **Trelawny**, is **Greenwood Great House**. Greenwood is one of a number of Great Houses scattered through the northern parishes that once belonged to the long-established Barrett family. Their connection with Jamaica dates back to 1655, the time of the English capture of the island when the first Barrett came with the forces of Penn and Venables. Greenwood was built about two hundred years ago and belonged to cousins of Elizabeth Barrett Browning, the famous 19th-century poet. The House has been renovated and furnished with antiques and is open to the public. As a special feature it has an unusual collection of antique musical instruments. Elizabeth Barrett Browning's

*The house, today a museum, preserves the original **Barrett family library**, some of the **paintings**, and one-of-a kind **pieces of furniture**.*

main family house in Jamaica was Cinnamon Hill Great House, now in private hands. Her father, Edward, was born in that house but left the island for England as a boy and never returned. His stern and morose character as an adult may have been caused by the financial losses he suffered when slavery was abolished. His daughter Elizabeth never visited Jamaica, but two of her brothers who came out at different times to run the family properties are buried in the family graveyard at Cinnamon Hill where generations of Barretts lie. In spite of the family losses, Elizabeth Barrett supported the emancipation of the slaves.

25

*On these two pages, views of the splendid **Harmony Cove**.*

HARMONY COVE

On the north coast, past **Falmouth** and **Duncans**, is another corner of paradise. **Harmony Cove** is still largely untouched by mass tourism, but recently it has become one of the most sought-after sites for the luxury tourist trade. Today its wild beauty is enchanting – tomorrow services and comfort will add to its lure.

MARTHA BRAE RIVER

A legend narrates the story of an Arawak Indian woman, a 'good witch' of the native population (enslaved and all but exterminated by the Spaniards) who lived on the banks of a river far from the rest of the population during the colonial era.

When the Spaniards were searching for the mythical treasure of the Arawaks they demanded to be taken to the witch, who, it was rumoured, knew where it was hidden. The witch took the Spaniards to a grotto, leading them to believe it was there they would find the cache. But then she suddenly disappeared, leaving the conquistadors alone and terrorised. As the Europeans searched for a way out, they were swept away by the river, whose waters the witch had magically channelled into the course they still follow today.

Martha Brae River is best-known today for its rafting.

DUNN'S RIVER FALLS

Drax Hall Polo Club is the last point of interest on the outskirts of **St. Ann's Bay**, and there is little of note between that and what must be one of the most photographed waterfalls in the world, **Dunn's River Falls**. Singly and in human chains, countless tourists have scrambled up the huge limestone staircase of these enchanting falls, and they all have photographs to prove it.

Before the days of expanding tourism, the beach was fairly unfrequented except on public holidays. A rough flight of steps led down from the road, and there were no amenities. Gradually, provision was made for the increasing crowds so that now, starting from the car park high above the shore, wellbuilt steps lead to a tunnel below the road and down to the beach. Would-be climbers buy a ticket there to climb the falls, with or without an official guide, and then work their way back up to the car park. Sometimes it can be hard work, especially when the flow of water is unusually heavy, but there are numerous points where climbers can leave the river and finish the trip on land. The total height of the falls is 600 feet (200 m), but few attempt the complete ascent.

Near the car park are the usual facilities for visitors as well as stalls and shops where curios, souvenirs and wood carvings are sold. There are also snack bars and a number of look-out spots where it is possible to follow the progress of the climbers as they struggle up the falls.

*Snaps of visitors trying their skills in climbs up **Dunn's River Falls**.*

OCHO RIOS

Ocho Rios is a misnomer. No one has ever identified eight rivers there. The name is probably a corruption of Los Chorreros, 'waterfalls,' which are numerous west of the town, **Dunn's River Falls** being the most spectacular.

Once a sleepy fishing village and a holiday spot for Kingstonians, Ocho Rios began to grow as a tourist resort in the 1950s. Gradually, new hotels and condominiums were built, and a long stretch of beach was developed with docking facilities for cruise ships. The town expanded east and west, shopping plazas spread and many crafts markets were set up. Today, more cruise ships call at Ocho Rios than at any other island port, and the fishing village has become a tourist town. There is plenty of night life and entertainment as well as good discos and a number of attractive restaurants outside the hotels.

*A view of **Ocho Rios and its port**, with **Turtle Beach Towers** in the background.*

*An aerial view of the white-sand **Turtle Beach**,*
one of the most captivating of the Ocho Rios strands.

Every kind of water sport is offered here: sailing, wind-surfing, jet-skiing, para-sailing. Snorkelling and scuba diving equipment is easily hired, and diving lessons are widely available. Deep-sea fishing trips can be arranged by the day, and it is sometimes possible to go out with a local fisherman in his canoe, powered by an outboard motor, for a night's fishing.

Leisurely trips in glass-bottomed boats take visitors along the coast for an effortless look at the coral reefs and their brilliant fish.

Other sports available in Ocho Rios include volleyball on the beach, tennis on first class courts, horseback riding – which may take the horse lover as far as the equestrian centre at **Chukka Cove** – and golf on the eighteen hole course at **Sandals Golf and Country Club**. Of course, there is always swimming in pools or the sea or, for the non-energetic, simply floating with the tide.

CRUISING

A cruise is doubtless the most comfortable and safe vacation mode: the many cruise ships that come ashore at Jamaica's ports every day are enormous, full-comfort vessels, true floating cities that depart ports all over the world to ply the Caribbean waters. Among the many stopover ports on the island, Ocho Rios is undoubtedly one of the favourites thanks to its welcoming atmosphere and the sheer beauty of its coastline.

Above, two light sailboats anchored off **Sandals Hotel**.

This page, right: impressive **Caribbean cruise ships** *in the Ocho Rios waters.*

DOLPHIN COVE

Imagine petting a friendly, playful dolphin in a magnificent cove with a fine white-sand beach. It isn't a dream - it's **Dolphin Cove**! The only place in Jamaica where you can benefit from the knowledge and advice of expert trainers and swim and frolic with dolphins under their watchful eye. But dolphins aren't the only attraction here: at Dolphin Cove you can also see other denizens of these exotic lands: parrots and other brightly-coloured tropical birds on land, and in the waters tropical fish, mantas, and the terrible sharks. Dolphin Cove truly has something for everyone!

Anyone who's been to Dolphin Cove will tell you that thanks to the animals' friendly nature and the trainers' warm welcome, their day with the dolphins was the highlight of their trip to Jamaica.

Dolphin Cove's attractions don't stop at the dolphins: you'll also enjoy touch encounters with land animals, listening to the music, and shopping for souvenirs.

PORT ANTONIO

With its twin harbours and **Navy Island** guarding the approaches, Port Antonio occupies the most beautiful site of any small town in Jamaica. The foothills of the **Blue Mountains** rise steeply behind the town, and the view from the **Bonnie View Hotel** hundreds of feet above is one of the finest in the world.

Port Antonio is one of the best centres for water sports in Jamaica. There is a marina on Navy Island and the **Admiralty Club** provides for a full range of marine activities. Some of the best snorkelling and scuba diving in Jamaican waters is off these shores. This is also the focus of activity for deep sea fishing. Blue marlin can be caught little more than a mile off shore, and the **Marlin Tournament** in October is an international event. A few miles along the coast past **San San Bay** is the **Blue Hole**, a good spot for water skiing but even better for diving. Reputed to be bottomless, it is, in fact, a little over 200 feet (70 m) deep, its great depth producing its intense, luminous blue colour.

The **Errol Flynn Property** lies further along the coast, and Mrs. Patricie Flynn welcomes visitors to this working plantation. Port Antonio is also the point of departure for those going rafting down the **Rio Grande**. This is an adventure that no one should miss.

Whether or not it is true that Errol Flynn organized raft races on the Rio Grande hardly matters now that rafting down the river has become one of the major tourist attractions of the North Coast.

First-time rafters may feel apprehensive when they see the long, frail-looking rafts with the river lapping between the lengths of bamboo, but it was rafts like these that carried heavy loads of bananas down to Port Antonio in the heyday of the banana export boom. Once on board the surprisingly stable rafts, travellers will soon feel secure in the care of the experienced raftsman. All the raftsmen have to serve a long apprenticeship – sometimes, as long as ten years – before they can be licensed to carry passengers.

*The splendid **Blue Lagoon**, a spectacularly beautiful expanse of water accessible from the sea and from a narrow road from the interior.*

RIO GRANDE

The **Rio Grande**, originally a practical route for the river dwellers to get their produce to market more quickly and in better condition than over the rugged local roads, is world famous for its rafting. Rafting down the Rio Grande can be an unforgettable experience. It's a dream voyage through a pristine landscape for those who are ready to sit back and absorb all it has to offer. Idyllic scenes may appear around any bend in the river, and one may come up on locals swimming, reminiscent of much earlier days when Arawak Indians fished and swam here and the whole island lived up to its name, Xaymaca, 'land of wood and water'.

*A relaxing dip in a sheltered bend of the **Rio Grande**.*

KINGSTON

The modern office blocks and hotels of **New Kingston**, the financial towers along the waterfront downtown, and the steady expansion of the city reflect the dynamic spirit of Kingston as it is now, a far cry from the colonial backwater it had become seventy years ago. Today, Kingston is a major Caribbean business and communications centre, the seat of the Government of Jamaica and a magnet for the whole island. In its sprawling growth, Kingston has

spread across the **Liguanea Plain** and up into the hills of **St. Andrew** to the north. From these hills, the houses of the well-to-do look down upon a green city, trees screening most of the buildings except the residential apartment blocks and commercial towers which punctuate the landscape. Even downtown Kingston, a series of crossroads crowded with minibuses, handcarts and top-heavy country buses, has its green corners which have escaped the jostling crowds. And the sea is always close at hand. Kingston never forgets that it is a port. Situated on one of the finest harbours in the world, with the **Caribbean Sea** washing its shore, it provides the most extensive trans-shipment facili-

ties in the Caribbean for vessels of all nations. Built after the destruction of **Port Royal** in the earthquake of 1692, Kingston was intended to be a commercial city. As a result, no impressive buildings were erected except for the **Kingston Parish Church**. This stood on the south side of the well laid-out grid system of streets and lanes on which the city was based.

Downtown Kingston still conforms to the original grid system but the city has spread far beyond the first limits. The prosperous move northward, while densely populated streets and yards fan out east and west of the old commercial centre, full of the life and activity of a growing city bursting out of its boundaries.

*Top inset, the **Kingston Parish Church** in downtown Kingston, a faithful reproduction of the original church destroyed by the 1907 earthquake.*

Kingston's Norman Manley International Airport (bottom inset), being renewed, is the ideal point of arrival for business and tourism, thanks to its proximity to Kingston and the historic centre of Port Royal.

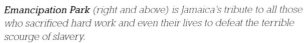

Emancipation Park *(right and above) is Jamaica's tribute to all those who sacrificed hard work and even their lives to defeat the terrible scourge of slavery.*

Bottom right, **Waterfront** *in downtown Kingston.*

Bottom, **Redemption Song** *located in Emancipation Park, a statue of two freed slaves, their eyes looking skyward in symbolic thanks for Jamaica's liberation from slavery.*

KINGSTON WATERFRONT

Although there are comparatively few of the usual tourist attractions in Kingston, three are to be found along the **Kingston Waterfront**. West of the **Bank of Jamaica**, which has a fascinating display of coins, is the **Government Conference Centre**, linked to the nearby **Oceana Hotel**, which is now used as an office building. Its **Conference Centre** is an interesting and attractive building, ideally suited to its function. The interior design makes refreshingly wide use of Jamaican crafts. A surprising discovery here is the very good lunch menu in the light and airy cafeteria.

Further along the Waterfront is the **Roy West Building** which now houses the **Jamaican National Gallery**. The works on display are of a quality and variety that reflect the wide scope of Jamaican artists and their multi-cultural background. One section of the Gallery is devoted to classical works of the past depicting Jamaican scenes and works with Jamaican connections.

At the far end of the Waterfront is the **Craft Market**. The covered market is filled with small streets of stalls and shops packed with straw goods and souvenirs. There are brightly embroidered straw baskets and mats, hats made of the fine *jippi-jappa* straw, baskets of coconut or banana fibres, wood carvings, trays inlaid with native wood, bongo drums, shakers, strings of beads, fine needlework, openwork dresses and jewelry. It is almost impossible to come away empty-handed.

DOWNTOWN

The statues of **Sir Alexander Bustamante** and **Norman Washington Manley** face in opposite directions to the north and south of **St. William Grant Park** in central Kingston. These men were the founders of Jamaica's two major political parties, and each played a significant and dominant role in preparing the country for Independence in 1962.

A **statue of Queen Victoria** once stood where Sir Alexander Bustamante's has ever since the monarch had to make way for the new age of independence. Sir Alexander's statue faces **Kingston Parish Church**, first built in the late 17th and early 18th centuries. It was completely destroyed in the earthquake of 1907 which, together with the subsequent fire, reduced most of Kingston to ruins. The new church was built exactly on the model of the old, and the clock tower was added after the **First World War** as a memorial to those Jamaicans who had died in battle. On the north side is the **Ward Theatre** standing on a site which for centuries featured a theatre. A gift to the people of Kingston by Colonel Ward, it is a fine example of late 19th-century theatre architecture.

*Facing page, top, the **Ward Theatre**, Kingston's historic venue for protagonists of national theatre and many international stars.*

*The **statues of Washington Manley** (top left) and **Sir Alexander Bustamante** (left), the founders of Jamaica's major political parties.*

*A must on any visit to Kingston is a stroll among the stalls of the craft market. On this page, several **handmade bags** in traditional colours and finely-crafted leather.*

CRAFT MARKET

Bottom on this page, some of the unnumbered articles on display in the **city market stalls**.

Intricate basket-weaving patterns and the colours of the **garments** and **accessories** are typical of Jamaican crafts.

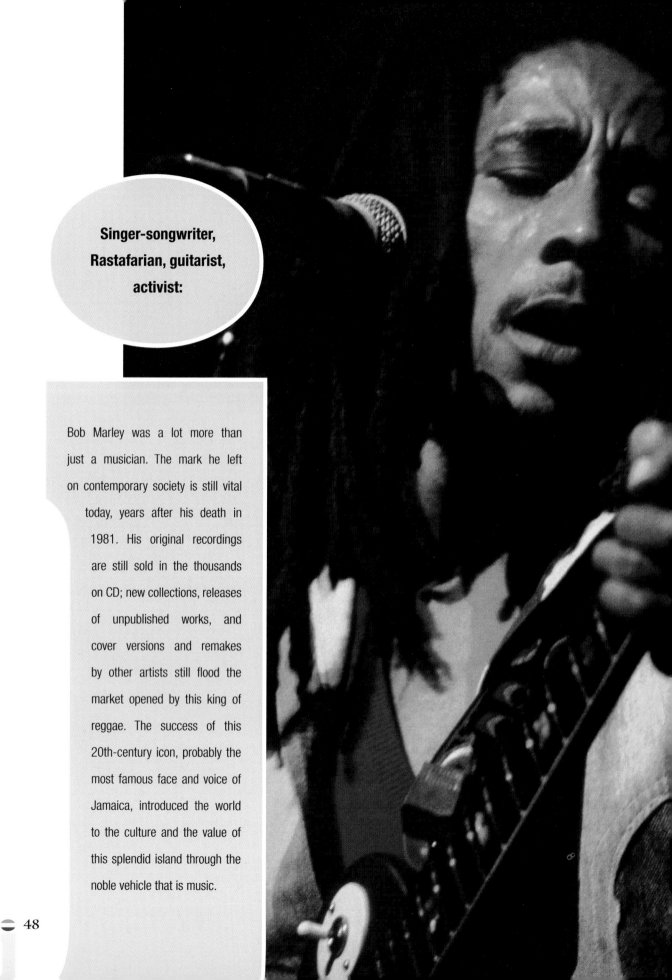

Singer-songwriter, Rastafarian, guitarist, activist:

Bob Marley was a lot more than just a musician. The mark he left on contemporary society is still vital today, years after his death in 1981. His original recordings are still sold in the thousands on CD; new collections, releases of unpublished works, and cover versions and remakes by other artists still flood the market opened by this king of reggae. The success of this 20th-century icon, probably the most famous face and voice of Jamaica, introduced the world to the culture and the value of this splendid island through the noble vehicle that is music.

BOB MARLEY
MUSEUM

This museum presents the life and successes of this extraordinary artist in a collection of memorabilia, artefacts, documents, photographs, and personal items. If you have a chance to go to Hope Road in Kingston, don't miss the museum, once upon a time **Bob Marley's home**. The two-story house is just as it was when the great reggae musician lived here.

*Above and bottom right, the **exterior of the museum**, decorated with Rasta colours.*

*On the facing page, a famous close-up of **Bob Marley** during a concert held in London in 1977.*

*Bottom left, a **musical event** uniting reggae, jazz, and blues.*

HOPE BOTANICAL GARDENS AND ZOO

Hope Zoo is the perfect place for a family outing. Wide-open spaces offer ideal living conditions for the animals and let curious visitors interact safely with the zoo's inhabitants. The zoo hosts animals that are found only in Jamaica, along with crocodiles, parrots, pink flamingoes and many other exotic birds, monkeys, lions, and many more. To cap your day, what could be better than a visit to the **Hope Botanical Gardens**, the most fascinating green space in all of Kingston, adjoining the zoo.

Some of the animals at **Kingston's Hope Zoo**. *Anti-clockwise from left: flamingoes, a lion, a crocodile, Jamaican patoos, a parrot.*

IGUANA

The **Jamaican iguana** is unique in the world. Growing to more than 150 cm in length, it is the largest land animal endemic to the island.

For a long time *Cyclura collei* was believed to be extinct, until several individuals were rediscovered. Now, thanks to the experts at Kingston's Hope Zoo, the endangered iguanas breed in captivity and are released into the wild.

DEVON HOUSE

Devon House is one of the best remaining examples of classical Jamaican architecture. It was built in 1881 by George Stiebel, a black Jamaican who had made his fortune overseas. Although it was once surrounded by extensive grounds, it is essentially a town house, with- out the large work-related and storage elements of the country Great Houses. However, it has many of the char- acteristic features of the old plantation houses; high ceil- ings, spacious rooms with plenty of accommodation for guests, wide verandahs and shining floors. It also had the traditional outside kitchen and bath-house, servants' quarters and stables.

*The magnificent gardens (above) and accurately furnished interiors (right) of **Devon House** attract thousands of tourists, as do the restaurants, shops, and other attractions nearby.*

JAMAICA HOUSE

Located north of **Devon House**, Jamaica House, built in 1960, is today the official seat of the offices of the Jamaican Prime Minister, but in the past was the residence of the Prime Minister and his family. More recently, the wife of a former Jamaican Prime Minister, Mrs. Beverley Anderson Manley (who went on to become a popular radio personality), founded the **Jamaica Basic School** in one of the mansion's annexes, in the hope the school would become a model for excellence in Jamaican education.

KING'S HOUSE

Before becoming the official residence of the Governor General. **King's House** was a church property: it was built as the residence of the Lord Bishop of Jamaica and purchased in 1871 to be made over into the Governor's mansion.

King's House hosts a number of works of inestimable value: portraits of King George III and Queen Charlotte by the famous artist Sir Joshua Reynolds. King's House has played host to many important figures in political life, including Prince Albert and Prince George (who later became George V), the Duke and Duchess of York (later George VI and his Queen), Princess Margaret, Her Majesty Queen Elizabeth II, and the Duke of Edinburgh.

King's House is open to the public; visitors can also have tea here as part of the Meet the People program. For more information, contact the **Jamaica Tourist Board**.

Below, **King's House**.

*Above, **Jamaica House** and the front garden.*

GORDON HOUSE

In 1960, **Gordon House** became the official meeting place of the **Jamaican government**. The building is named for the national hero George William Gordon, promoter of freedom and justice for all social classes. In the 1850s, Gordon was elected to the House of Assembly and acquired a reputation as a defender of the rights of the former slaves: although abolished in 1838, slavery had left a weighty legacy of discrimination. Gordon's strong activism led to his being sentenced to death under martial law. He is now considered a national hero in the fight against discrimination.

*Below, the modern lines of **Gordon House**.*

PORT ROYAL

For the visitor, **Fort Charles** is the major attraction in **Port Royal**. The solid brick walls and the guns still look threatening. It was named after King Charles when he came to the English throne in 1660, as was the town itself. The first of three forts defending the town, it was the only one to survive the 1692 earthquake. Now there is a small **Maritime Museum** within its walls. Once a year, the fort is the venue for a splendid costume party, the **Port Royal Revels**, attended by buccaneers and their wenches in their finery, part of the fund-raising activities for the rebuilding of the town. Port Royal remained a defence station until comparatively recent times. A reminder of those days is an old artillery arsenal tilted into the sand by the 1907 earthquake which destroyed Kingston. The hundred-year old building is called the **Giddy House**, and anyone who walks inside is likely to suffer from a sudden attack of vertigo. One of the oldest buildings in Port Royal is **St. Peter's Anglican Church**. The church, erected in 1725, replaced two earlier ones. The first was demolished in the 1692 earthquake and the second was destroyed in the fire of 1703. The present church was not finally completed until 1926.

The inside of the church is notable for its magnificent wood-work, some of it from ships' timbers. The organ loft dates back to 1743. On the walls are memorials to those who are buried in the church, some of them very young soldiers and sailors who were struck down

*On this page, the walls and cannons of **Fort Charles**.*

by the fevers which repeatedly broke out among the garrison. The church silver is reputed to be the gift of Henry Morgan himself. It is possible to see the tankard, covered chalice, and two patens which he supposedly gave, and they certainly date back to the 17th century. There have been repeated attempts to find the treasures of Port Royal. Archaeological work has discov-

ered many artifacts which tell the story of every-day life three hundred years ago but it is unlikely that much of great value will be recovered. Hardly had the shocks of the first earthquake subsided before the more intrepid were going down in primitive diving bells to see what riches they could retrieve from the ruins. Whatever was easily accessible would have

St. Peter's Anglican Church: views of the interiors, details, and a view of the exterior.

been scavenged then, and the rest must have long since vanished. The recent finds are fascinating. Many of them are on display in the **Archaeological Museum** in the old **Naval Hospital** just outside the town. The museum gives a detailed picture of life in Port Royal

and the disaster. The exhibits include a hoard of clay pipes, a silver pocket watch which stopped at 11:39, the time of the earthquake, pieces of eight, masses of household objects and a beautiful porcelain statue of a Chinese goddess.

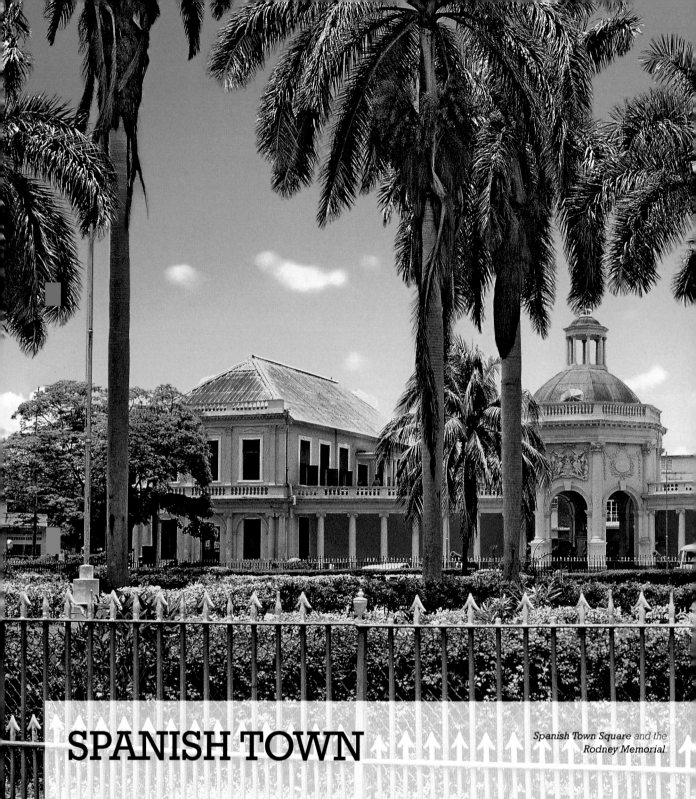

SPANISH TOWN ↟↟↟↟↟↟↟↟↟

Spanish Town Square and the Rodney Memorial.

For three hundred and fifty years, **Spanish Town** was the centre of Jamaican government. The Spanish founded it in 1523 when Sevilla la Nueva on the North Coast proved to be unsuitable. The new town, Villa de la Vega, flourished and by the time of the English capture in 1655 was an attractive, well-built capital. Not one of the Spanish buildings remains today. The English destroyed some of the houses, but more were flattened by the earthquake of 1692 and there was further destruction by a hurricane in 1713.

The handsome brick building with the long arched colonnade is the old **House of Assembly**, built in 1762 and now used as government offices. Across the square is the façade of the **Old King's House**, all that remains after the building was gutted by fire in 1925.

JAMAICAN PEOPLE'S MUSEUM OF CRAFT AND TECHNOLOGY

The former stables at the back of **Old King's House** have become the home of a collection of relics which give a vivid picture of a past and passing way of life, from goods sold in the village shop to agricultural tools. Old cooking utensils such as the yabbas, clay bowls, and the cassava graters shown here have almost completely disappeared from use. Many items show a remarkable ingenuity in turning whatever materials are on hand into tools and utensils.

Nearby there is a collection of ancient horse-drawn vehicles including an old mobile fire engine. Obviously it could have been of little use in controlling the recurrent fires which plagued Spanish Town.

CASTLETON GARDENS

Travelling to the North Coast from Kingston usually means taking one of two spectacular routes. The **A1** bypasses **Spanish Town** and continues over **Mount Diablo** to **Ocho Rios**.

The **A3**, or **Junction Road**, runs further east and is the route usually taken for Port Antonio. It was the last major road opened to the North Coast, when the growth of banana exports from Port Antonio in the late 1800s spurred construction of a quicker, more reliable route to Kingston. Cutting a road to follow the winding Wag Water River was a major feat of engineering, but finally the old road was extended from **Castleton Gardens** over the river to the coast. The new stretch is full of hairpin bends and breathtaking scenery.

Castleton Gardens, among the first botanical gardens in the western hemisphere, were established in 1862 on 15 acres of riverside land some 13 miles north of Kingston. Official guides show visitors around the Gardens, pointing out rare specimens and happily demonstrating the unusual effect of the Silver-Leaf Fern. The Gardens are a popular picnic spot for Kingstonians.

*Some views of the luxuriantly green **Castleton Gardens**.*

FERN GULLY

Taking the **A1** route out of **Kingston** also means following a road with some difficult sections. After the old **Flat Bridge**, across the **Rio Cobre**, the **Bog Walk Gorge**, and the steep, twisting climb up **Mount Diablo**, the road winds down towards the sea. Some five miles (8 km) south of Ocho Rios, it plunges into the deep shade and greenery of **Fern Gully**, once a river bed and still requiring caution in heavy rain. For four miles it meanders through lush tropical growth before emerging into sunlight just above Ocho Rios and the sea.

*The A1 route offers a unique opportunity to view more **500 different species of ferns**.*

TREASURE BEACH AND LOVERS' LEAP

Treasure Beach.
*Right, **Lovers' Leap**, and, bottom, the lighthouse.*

The southwestern coast of Jamaica is the other face of this charming island, the side made of small fishermen's communities, quiet paths, and local legends. Places like **Treasure Beach** take us back in time to taste what travel was before the era of the mass tourism boom in the Caribbean islands. Here, you can still find semi-deserted beaches and small, hospitable villages where you can make friends with the sociable people of the area.

Not far from Treasure Beach is the romantic **Lovers' Leap** lighthouse. For centuries it has been narrated how a couple of young, enamoured slaves chose to throw themselves to their deaths over this cliff in one of the island's most beautiful panoramic points, against the endless sky, rather than endure separation after sale to two masters.

YS FALLS

When the falls were opened to the public in 1990 they became an immediate success. What makes this such a popular attraction is that it is completely natural. Seven separate falls create an elegant scenario around small green pools in which visitors can take a relaxing dip in complete safety. Lifeguards show visitors where it is safe to swim and suggest the most suitable falls for each bather. One of the natural falls is perfect for children and for non-swimmers – or visitors who just want to sit quietly in the water.

For children there is also a play space where parents can park them while they browse in the craft shop at the entrance or take the guided tour on a small bus to discover the other marvels of this corner of paradise.

On these pages, visitors in the incredibly beautiful scenario of **YS Falls**.

BLACK RIVER

For years now an interesting form of eco-tourism has been developing along Jamaica's longest watercourse, the **Black River**. Tour operators conduct safaris on the delta and the **Great Morass**. The most interesting facet of these safaris, which permit the visitor to observe firsthand the rich flora and fauna of the habitats near the mangrove forests, is that they are conducted in the territory of the more than 300 remaining examples of the American Crocodile.

Once much more numerous, the crocodiles are nearing extinction following years of uncontrolled hunting for their skins, used in manufacturing fashion accessories. The American Crocodile is now a protected species in Jamaica.

The safari safeguards the interests of the crocodiles . . . and the visitors alike. The 'croc safaris' travel in safe motor launches and the captains/tour guides are expert navigators. And they have even named some of the more 'personable' crocodiles!

BLUEFIELDS

O ur journey along the South Coast is almost at its end. But first, a last stop at **Bluefields**, an uncontaminated corner of Jamaica where we can meet the local people, taste Jamaican home-cooking, and explore sites with long, rich histories. Bluefields, once known as Oristan, was the third colonial settlement in Jamaica. Unfortunately, the only remaining relic of the distant past is a single cannon, dated 1520, at the historical site.

*Bathers at **Bluefields Beach Park**.*
Above, local women selling fried fish and shrimp.

NEGRIL

At the farthest western end of the island, **Negril** was once nothing more than a tiny fishing village and a lighthouse. In the fifties, good roads were built and the area began to be opened up. Enterprising Kingstonians began to make the long journey to Negril for holidays and the fame of **Negril Beach**, seven miles of white sand sloping gently into a crystal clear sea, began to spread. One or two modest hotels were built. Suddenly, in the late 1960s, Negril began to be discovered by the young 'me generation', the hippies and followers of the counterculture. They arrived in Montego Bay only to leave it as quickly as possible and make for

*The enchantment of the sparkling white sand of **Seven Mile Beach**.*

the laid-back life of Negril. Local people opened up their homes to the visitors. Some accommodation was little more than a hammock and a thatched roof, and nude bathing and marijuana smoking became part of the Negril way of life for many.

Today, things have changed. Not that Negril has lost its totally relaxed atmosphere, but life is more structured; there are more hotels, tourist bungalows and organised entertainment. Since tourism started from the ground up in this part of Jamaica, relationships between visitors and locals are different here. Residents mingle freely with tourists who are far more a part of local life than they are along the North Coast.

Sun, sand and sea. These are what Negril has to offer. Incredibly white sands, a brilliant sea ranging through an indescribable spectrum of jewel colours, and long

hours of sunshine. Add to these a way of life close to nature and an easy acceptance of people of all kinds, and the sum total is the perfect place to escape from the stresses of metropolitan life.

At the northern end of Negril Beach is **Bloody Bay**, famous as the spot where the notorious pirate Calico Jack and his crew were captured in 1720 and shipped to Kingston for execution. Fishermen use this beach as well as the southern end of Negril Beach and the whole length of the shore is a well-travelled right of way for holiday-makers, local workers and whoever prefers the seashore to the high road.

Jamaican faces, often smiling, reflect the multiple racial strains of their history. Most of the population is black, the inheritance of the days of slavery, but those days also brought a British, especially Scottish and Irish, ancestry. From Europe came Jews and Catholics, as well as Germans, who settled in the south of the island. In the 19th century, Indians and Chinese came as indentured labour. Many of them stayed and went into business. To this day, some of the sugar growing areas have a population with a higher proportion of Indian descent than the national average. Later still, merchants came from Lebanon and Syria. Together, they represent the national motto, Out of Many One People. And, as a people, Jamaicans have a very high standard of good looks. So far, three Jamaicans have won the Miss World crown.

Some characteristic Negril sites: **Royal Palm Reserve** *(top), the* **lighthouse** *(left),* **West End Cliff** *(bottom, from Pirates Cave), and the* **Negril Hills Golf Club** *(facing page, top).*

SANDALS NEGRIL

J amaica's longest beach, the world-famous **Seven Mile**, is home to the splendid **Sandals Negril**.

The resort, with its marvellous spa, features true beachfront rooms. Guests can spend a lazy day in the shade of the palms, literally a step away from the sands . . .

PIRATES CAVE

This corner of Negril is the ideal spot for adding a touch of verve to your vacation. The waters are protected by the barrier cliffs where, centuries ago, pirates and buccaneers safely anchored their ships out of sight of the authorities. Today, if you're a diving buff, you can even go in search of their lost treasures in the caves! But if you prefer dizzying heights to submarine depths, you'll enjoy the **Pirates Cave cliff**, a truly spectacular diving platform.

*Visitors to **Pirates Cave** diving from the cliff (top and facing page), enjoying a dip (below), and relaxing at the cliff-side bar on the sea (bottom left).*

SAILING IN JAMAICA

The most adventurous way to discover Jamaica is to follow its coasts aboard a luxury yacht, a light boat, a nimble catamaran . . . or a sailing ship!
Many of the island's **tourist ports** rent vessels of various tonnage for a relaxing day of fishing or for exploring the coastline from a new and different perspective . . . from the sea.

Old and new vessels ply the Jamaican seas.

JAMAICA, A LAND OF TRADITION

CRAFTS

Crafts express the soul of a people. Crafts can capture the symbols and forms of tradition and give them new and different expressions in objects and other creations. Tradition is magically transformed in the hands of each single craftsperson into *objets d'art*. Jamaican crafts are certainly no exception: the variety of symbols, products, and materials mirrors the thousand faces of this great island. Along your travel itinerary you'll see no end of market stalls selling baskets, accessories, prints, toys, objects for the home, and an infinity of other original items.

Of particular interest are the **wooden statues** that incorporate the symbols and the myriad faces of Jamaica, the masks, objects woven from the straw and cane, and the brilliantly-coloured fabrics of the islands.

SHELL WORK

A̲ll things considered, they're really only the 'houses' of many species of molluscs – but the unique forms and incredible geometrical perfection of **shells** have always tempted collectors and beach-combing tourists looking for a souvenir that can 'house' their memories of a special vacation.

In the shops along the beachfront and in the island's craft markets you'll find may large shells with the strangest and most bizarre shapes. And if you take one home with you . . . and if you become nostalgic on a cold winter's day, just put the shell to your ear and you'll again hear the sound of the Jamaican surf and the wind on the waves.

*You'll find **bars** (bottom left) and **crafts shops** (above) almost everywhere along Jamaica's coasts, often just a few meters from the beach. Below, a **display of conch shells**.*

*As the photos on the facing page show, many **Jamaican craft workshops** are open for the public to watch the artisans at work and admire their displays of finished products.*

*A local dancer in **traditional dress** performing for the public in a night club.*

FOLK DANCE

Dance is a fundamental reality in Jamaica, one that exactly mirrors the soul of Jamaican culture, which incorporates European tradition but only through the filter of African culture.

For example, traditional European dances like the quadrille have undergone radical transformation and over time become something quite different and uniquely Jamaican. Other dances, instead, are of African origin, like the *gerreh* or the *ettu*. They have always been expressions of farm life on the plantations, and for centuries they accompanied the life of many Jamaicans, slaves and fieldworkers.

As we travel in Jamaica we will inevitably come into contact with one or another form of dance, whether on occasion of a cultural event, at a party, or even on the street, in an impromptu celebration.

SUGAR CANE, COCONUT AND COFFEE

These plants–not surprisingly the mainstays of the Jamaican food and drink – are widely distributed throughout the island.

For centuries present on Jamaican soil, they have beaten out not only the mealtimes of the Jamaican families but indeed the lives of entire generations involved in their cultivation on the plantations.

Coconut is the only truly autochthonous – that is, indigenous – plant among the three. **Coffee**, instead, was imported centuries ago from Ethiopia, in Africa, as were many of the slaves employed as farm workers by the Spanish colonisers. The Spaniards also imported **sugar cane**, the plant that gives us rum, the liquor that has come to symbolise the Caribbean islands.

*Above, **Kingston coffee pickers** at work.*
*Bottom, the **Bernard Lodge Sugar Factory**.*

*Top, **jelly coconuts**.*
*Right, a **raft captain** carves a drawing
on a Jamaican gourd for visitors.*

FLORA

Clockwise from the top, **Jamaican Oak** *(Catalpa longissima),*
Blue Snakeweed *(Stachytarpheta jamaicensis),*
and **Brunfelsia jamaicensis**.

JAMAICAN FLOWERS

Despite the fact that since Spanish colonial times much of the island's land has been put to agricultural use, there are still many areas where spontaneous vegetation grows luxuriantly, especially in the extensive forests in the mountainous, wild areas of the interior. Thanks to the tropical climate, especially rainy in the north, more than **3000 flowering species** proliferate in Jamaica, including many varieties of **orchids** and **bougainvilleas**, Solanaceae, and the lignum vitae (*Guaiacum officinale*), the national flower.

A curious fact: about one hundred of the species that flourish in Jamaica are unique to the island; that is, they are found nowhere else on the entire earth. Some of the most common species are illustrated below.

JAMAICAN OAK

Catalpa longissima (Jacq.) Dum.-Cours.
(Bignoniaceae)

The genus name *Catalpa* derives from *carawba*, the name given the plants by the native populations of the southern United States. The genus is widely distributed, from North America to China and Tibet and also in some Caribbean islands; the species *C. longissima*, native to Jamaica (where it is known as the Jamaican Oak), Haiti and Martinique, is a tree to 25 meters with fissured-reticulate grey bark. The leathery leaves are ovate-elliptical, occasionally obovate, with entire but slightly undulate margins. The corolla of the tubular flowers is 2 to 3 cm in diameter, and yellowish-white blushed pink with striations that are purple on the outside and yellow within.

*Although its use is prohibited by law, **cannabis** has become a symbol of Jamaica, in part thanks to reggae music, generally linked to the Rastafari movement which encourages its use for facilitating meditation. The label in the photograph provides a summary medical/scientific analysis of the plant.*

BRUNFELSIA JAMAICENSIS

Brunfelsia jamaicensis Griseb.
(No Common English Name)
(Solanaceae)

B. *jamaicensis* Griseb. is distributed in the tree-studded savannas on the majority of the Caribbean islands, but it was first discovered on Jamaica; hence the species epithet. This plant is very similar to *B. plicata*, also discovered on Jamaica, and the two can be confidently treated as a single species. *B. jamaicensis* is a low shrub to 1.5 meters with branches that are minutely pubescent especially when young. The oblong-lanceolate obtuse leaves are first membranous, then leathery, with prominent veinings. The flowers are white when they first open and later become yellowish in colour; they may be as wide across as 6 cm; pedicels at most one cm in length support the slender tube.

BLUE SNAKEWEED

Stachytarpheta jamaicensis
(L.) M. Vahl
(Verbenaceae)

This herb grows to one meter in open areas and along the roadsides, with creeping stems that are, however, erect in the distal portion. The ovate-elliptical leaves are 2 by 7 cm in size, with dentate margins. The flowers, which range in colour from violet to blue, open only a few at a time in erect inflorescences as long as 20 cm. For more than two centuries, this herb has been a mainstay of folk medicine in treatment of dermal fungus infections, diarrhea and diabetes, and as a laxative. It is also eaten raw as a salad green.

MANGROVE

The mangrove forests or swamps represent a type of vegetation formation that usually develops along the low coastlines but may also reach inland, as far as ecological conditions permit. The term 'mangrove' actually stands for a group of plants, trees, shrubs and palms that all exhibit morphological adaptations such as to make them suitable for living in areas with muddy soils that are constantly flooded by water more or less rich in chloride salts, and in which the moving water itself is a constant source of disturbance. These factors obviously set serious limits to plant life, and the plants that live in similar habitats have reacted by evolving various structural modifications and reproductive strategies that permit them to variously deal with each.

Swamps are habitats of exceptional naturalistic interest for the great number of species they support, and in absolute terms the habitats containing the greatest biodiversity found anywhere in nature, since here freshwater, saltwater, and terrestrial species coexist with other species capable of exploiting all these types of environments. The naturalist's concern for conservation, however, is not the only argument supporting the need to guarantee protection for this type of habitat: just think that about 75% of the species of commercial value to the fishing industry pass at least a part of their life cycle in these habitats. These forested wetlands are also of fundamental importance for defending the coasts from erosion, since they are capable of absorbing the energy of the tides and the winds. This type of vegetation is also essential for the life of the **coral barrier reefs**, since its intricate root system catches terrigenous sediments before they can reach the reef where they would seriously jeopardize the very existence of the corals, which depend on clear water for their survival. What is more, by holding back the sediments, the mangrove roots act as filters for polluting agents - thus keeping the coastal waters clean.

*The **mangrove forests** are particular types of vegetation formations that are always densely overgrown. Right and left, **mangrove habitats**. Top, a detail of a **flower** in a mangrove forest.*

DIVING

A boundless **coral reef**, formations of gorgonids and sponges, varied and brightly-coloured undersea fauna. Diving in Jamaica is a unique experience.

Many divers adventure into the depths of the Jamaican waters in search of buccaneers' treasure, and while they'll probably never find a sunken galleon loaded with gold doubloons, they are likely to discover underwater grottoes containing treasures of another kind: a wealth of underwater flora and fauna. There are **many grottoes** in the Jamaican waters, and are often only a short distance from the diving centres, where the aspiring diver will find equipment and expert instructors. Guided diving tours take you there to observe the colourful fish of the Caribbean or even meet a group of dolphins for a playful romp in the water. Just a few of the many diving centres, names that will have a familiar ring to enthusiasts of Jamaican scuba diving, are: **Coral Seas Garden** (Negril), **Millie the Moray**, **Rock Cliff Reef**, **Giant Pillar Coral**, **The Arch**, and **Throne Room**.

SEA TURTLES

These marvellous animals, among the world's oldest, swim untiringly through the world's oceans for hundreds of kilometres.

The **adult females** of the species lay their eggs, about one hundred at a time, in solitude on the same beach where they themselves were hatched. The hatching of turtles' eggs and the hatchlings' run to the sea is probably one of the most thrilling shows in all nature.

Tourists offered turtle egg shells of other parts of turtles as souvenirs should remember that commerce in sea turtles, whether dead or alive, is strictly illegal! Just as it is illegal to even possess such items.

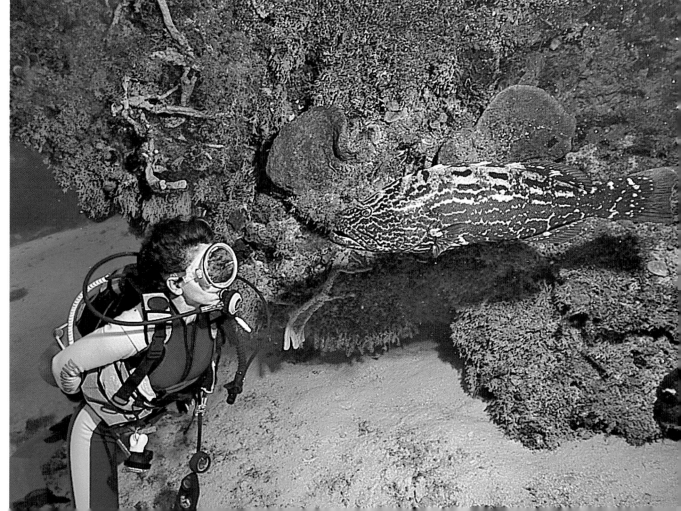

FOOD

The Jamaican day begins with a hearty meal: tropical fruit juice, toast, tea, and the classic dishes of a typical Jamaican breakfast: *ackee* and saltfish. If your day continues on the beach or strolling down Jamaica's streets, finding a snack or quick lunch is no problem.

Many kiosks sell fresh fruit and fast food. The national dish is *ackee* and saltfish (dried salted cod). Ackee is a tree imported from Africa centuries ago, with a beautiful and poisonous fruit. To be edible, it has to be picked, processed, and cooked by experts, and we therefore suggest trying *ackee* only at a restaurant or if prepared by an expert local cook. Another common dish is jerk pork: pork flavoured with spices and chili pepper and smoked or roasted to tenderness. Jamaican cuisine includes an incredible variety of grilled foods, from smoked ham to corn on the cob. Another typical and omnipresent food is – of course – fish, grilled or cooked in any number of other ways. Below are two exotic but easy to prepare recipes for a touch of Jamaica at home!

CURRIED REGGAE RICE SALAD
Makes 6 servings

Chef's notes: Make up to 1 day ahead. Garnish with avocado only when ready to serve, to keep it from browning.

Ingredients

1 large, ripe avocado, cubed when ready to serve
¾ cup long grain rice
1 tablespoon curry powder
½ garlic clove, crushed
4 scallions, chopped
1 stalk celery, diced
¼ cup each diced red, green,

yellow bell pepper
12 Greek olives, pitted, coarsely chopped
¼ cup golden raisins
¼ cup toasted walnuts, coarsely chopped
¼ cup grated coconut, fresh or dried
2 hard-boiled eggs, chopped

Dressing:
½ cup mayonnaise
3 tablespoons mango chutney (Major Grey's is excellent)
1 tablespoon creamy peanut butter
juice of one lime
¼ cup plain yogurt
salt and pepper to taste

1. Bring salted water to boil and cook rice about 15 minutes until all water is absorbed and the rice is tender. Stir in curry powder halfway through cooking.
2. Place in large glass bowl and refrigerate for 2 hours.
3. In blender, purée dressing ingredients. Chill in refrigerator.
4. Remove rice bowl from refrigerator and fold in remaining salad ingredients. Be careful not to mash up the eggs too much.
5. Pour dressing over salad and toss gently.
6. Sprinkle avocado with lemon juice to keep it from turning brown and use as garnish. Serve at once. Season with additional salt if needed.

HEY MON! JERK CHICKEN
Makes 8 servings

Chef's notes: Make the rub as hot or mild as you like it. Substitute milder chili peppers for the *habaneros*. Paste may be stored, tightly covered, in refrigerator for up to 2 weeks. Jerk seasoning can be easily purchased almost anywhere in Jamaica.

Ingredients
Chicken:
8 whole chicken legs
juice of 3 limes
1 teaspoon salt
oil for brushing grates of grill

Paste:
½ cup minced scallions
½ cup minced yellow onion
2 *habanero* peppers, seeded and minced
2 tablespoons freshly grated ginger
2 teaspoons fresh thyme leaves
1 teaspoon freshly ground allspice
1 teaspoon freshly black pepper
¼ teaspoon ground nutmeg
1 teaspoon ground cinnamon
1 tablespoon brown sugar
¼ cup red wine vinegar
3 tablespoons soy sauce
2 tablespoons olive oil
1 tablespoon salt

To make the paste
1. Combine all ingredients for paste in a food processor. Blend until smooth. Refrigerate.
To prepare the chicken
1. Rinse chicken legs under cold water and pat dry.
2. Place legs in large bowl and rub with lime juice and salt. Pour the paste over the chicken legs and rub in. Wear rubber gloves for this as the hot peppers contain volatile oils that can irritate skin. Cover and refrigerate 8 to 24 hours.
3. Brush cooking grate with oil and bring grill to medium heat. Grill chicken indirectly, turning now and then, until done. Meat will be opaque and juice will run clear – about 40 minutes.

COCKTAILS

JAMAICAN COCKTAIL

3/4 oz lime juice
1/2 oz coffee liqueur
3/4 oz dark rum
1 dash bitters

Shake the ingredients with ice cubes and serve in a chilled cocktail glass with a twist of lime peel.

BIG BAMBOO

2 oz rum
1 oz orange juice
1 oz pineapple juice
3/4 oz syrup
1 oz lemon juice
1/2 Triple sec

Shake and serve with fresh mint leaves.

JAMAICA RUM PUNCH

1 oz sugar
4 oz water
1 oz lime juice
3 oz Jamaican White Rum
1 oz strawberry syrup

Mix the lemon juice, sugar, syrup, and water until the sugar dissolves. Add the rum and serve over cracked ice. Decorate with hot red pepper.

NO PROBLEM

1/2 oz blue Curacao
1/2 oz lime juice
1 oz vodka
1 oz any fruit syrup

Shake with lots of ice and serve immediately topped with a whole fresh strawberry.

INDEX